Chocolate!

Diana Noonan

Contents

A World of Chocolate

What is the best **invention** ever?
Is it the car?
Is it the computer?
Is it **chocolate**?

We eat
chocolate.

We drink it.

We cook with it.

We give it as a gift.

Most of us love chocolate.

3

A Chocolate Tree?

Chocolate does not grow on trees. But chocolate is made from cocoa beans. Cocoa beans come from **cacao** trees.

Cocoa beans are seeds.
They grow in **pods**
on the cacao tree.

pod

The pods grow
on the trunk
and branches of
the cacao tree.

cacao tree

Workers pick the cocoa pods from the tree. They cut open the pods and take out the beans.
Then the beans are dried in the sun.

pod

bean

When they are dry, the cocoa beans are put into bags. Ships take the bags all over the world. Trucks take the bags to chocolate **factories**.

In some countries, cacao farmers are very poor. When you buy Fairtrade chocolate, you know that the farmers have been paid a fair price for their work.

A Famous Book about Chocolate

Films have also been made of *Charlie and the Chocolate Factory*.

Charlie and the Chocolate Factory is a very famous book. In the book, Charlie meets Willy Wonka who owns a chocolate factory.

Willy Wonka keeps his chocolate **recipes** a secret. But **spies** from other chocolate factories try to steal them.

Secret Recipes

Real chocolate factories keep their recipes a secret too. At one chocolate factory, a machine broke. A person came to fix the machine. He had to wear a **blindfold** as he walked in and out of the factory. This was to make sure he did not see any chocolate secrets!

You can visit chocolate factories. You can see how chocolate is made. You can even eat the chocolate. But the recipes are secret!

How Chocolate Is Made

This is what happens inside a chocolate factory. First the cocoa beans are roasted. This helps to bring out the chocolate taste.

Then a machine crushes the roasted beans into bits. Their shells come off.

roasting the beans   shells come off

The broken cocoa bits are called nibs.
The nibs are crushed into chocolate
paste. The paste is used
to make different
kinds of chocolate.

chocolate paste

nibs

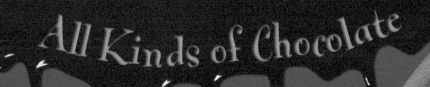

Cocoa is made from pressed and dried chocolate paste.

Cooking chocolate is made from cooled chocolate paste.

Dark chocolate is made from chocolate paste, **cocoa butter** and sugar.

Milk chocolate is made from chocolate paste, cocoa butter, sugar and milk.

There are many kinds of chocolate shapes and chocolate blocks.

This is a chocolate block. You may have eaten chocolate like this.

Chocolate is melted and tipped into special **moulds** to make shapes. Perhaps you have eaten a **white chocolate** rabbit!

This rabbit is made of white chocolate.

Yum!

The chocolate is being poured into a mould.

Imagine drinking chocolate from a chocolate fountain. Look at all the runny chocolate.

Yum!

Have you eaten chilli chocolate? Chocolate is yummy but chillies are hot! What would it be like to eat **spicy** chocolate?

There is also chocolate that has pepper in it!

Achoo!

The Chocolate Hall of Fame

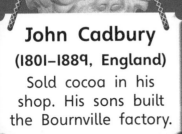

John Cadbury
(1801–1889, England)
Sold cocoa in his shop. His sons built the Bournville factory.

Henri Nestlé
(1814–1890, Switzerland)
Worked with a chocolate maker to make milk chocolate

These chocolate makers are famous.
They started making chocolate long ago.
Today, their names are still on chocolate
bar wrappers!

Rodolphe Lindt
(1855–1909, Switzerland)
Made extra-smooth chocolate

Milton Hershey
(1857–1945, USA)
Found a way to make
cheaper chocolate.
Built a chocolate
factory in 1905

Chocolate Bites

Every part of this pizza is made of chocolate, even the cheese!

Tasty Joke

Q: Why did the chocolate chip cookie go to the doctor?
A: Because it was feeling crummy.

The biggest chocolate egg ever made was 8 metres high. It weighed as much as a family car!

Chocolate Quiz

How much can you remember about chocolate?

1 Cocoa beans are:
  a chocolate beans
  b seeds
  c fruit

2 Dark chocolate is:
  a made with milk
  b made with dark-coloured cocoa beans
  c made without milk

3 Chocolate is shaped in:
  a moulds
  b tins
  c bottles

Glossary

blindfold	material tied over your eyes
cacao	small tree that grows in tropical areas
cocoa butter	fat pressed from the cocoa beans
cooking chocolate	chocolate with a stronger taste, used in baking
factories	buildings with equipment for making things
invention	clever idea or discovery
moulds	hollow shapes made of plastic or metal
paste	smooth, soft mixture
pods	outer covering for seeds
recipes	directions for cooking something
spicy	with a strong taste
spies	people who steal secret information
white chocolate	chocolate made from cocoa butter, milk and sugar